The Bean Trees

BookCaps™ Study Guide
<u>www.bookcaps.com</u>

© 2012. All Rights Reserved.

Table of Contents

ABOUT BOOKCAPS...**71**

Historical Context

Author Barbara Kingsolver grew up in eastern Kentucky and currently resides outside of Tucson, Arizona with her husband and two children. Her experiences in these two respective locations laid the foundation for *The Bean Trees*, which documents the migration of a young woman from her small town in Kentucky to Tucson.

The Bean Trees was published in 1988 and is Barbara Kingsolver's first novel. Since writing *The Bean Trees*, Kingsolver has gone on to publish nearly a dozen other books including *The Poisonwood Bible* and *Pigs in Heaven*, which is a sequel to *The Bean Trees*. Kingsolver has won multiple awards including the Dayton Literary Peace Prize and the Orange Prize for Fiction. She has been nominated for the Pulitzer Prize and the PEN/Faulkner Award.

Plot Summary

The Bean Trees tells the story of Taylor Greer, formerly Marietta "Missy" Greer, and her journey of self-discovery as she travels from rural Kentucky to bustling Tucson, Arizona. When Taylor initially sets out from her small town in Pittman County, she promises herself two things: that she will change her name and that she will stop to live wherever her car breaks down. The first promises she keeps; the second she doesn't. When her car breaks down in the middle of Oklahoma Cherokee country, Taylor can't imagine making such a place her home. She decides to get her car repaired and continue her journey. However, just before Taylor heads out, she encounters an Indian woman who insists Taylor take a young girl with her. Before Taylor can refuse, the woman is gone, and a bewildered Taylor is stuck with a little girl.

Taylor and the girl, whom Taylor names Turtle, continue their journey until Taylor's car breaks a second time in Tucson, Arizona. This time around, Taylor decides to stay. She meets an older woman named Mattie who own a tire shop and helps smuggle in and protect illegal immigrants from South America. Mattie soon becomes a close friend of Taylor's and even convinces Taylor to take a job at the tire store.

After looking through the roommate ads in the local paper, Taylor meets up with another Kentucky woman—Lou Ann. Lou Ann has an infant boy named Dwayne Ray and has been looking for company since her husband Angel left her and joined up with a rodeo. She invites Taylor and Turtle to move in. Although they have their share of disagreements, the two soon become close friends.

As Taylor and Turtle settle into life in Tucson, they meet many fascinating people including their neighbors Edna and Virgie Mae, and an immigrant couple from Guatemala, Estevan and Esperanza. Taylor becomes particularly close to Estevan, who tells her about the traumas he and his wife experienced in Guatemala including losing their daughter to the police. Around this time, Taylor brings Turtle to the doctor, where she receives the shocking news that Turtle was abused so severely as a baby that she developed a condition called "failure to thrive." Turtle is actually around three years old, even though she looks and acts like she could be two.

The climax of the story comes when Turtle is almost molested a second time when a man attacks her while she is walking in the park with Edna. Turtle reverts to not speaking again, and Taylor fears she may have lost all the progress she had previously made. The incident also brings Turtle's situation to the attention of a social worker. The social worker tells Taylor that without evidence and a formal adoption, she has no legal right to keep Turtle as her daughter. Meanwhile, Estevan and Esperanza risk discovery and deportation as immigration tensions rise in Arizona. Taylor ends up taking them on a road trip to Oklahoma so that they can move to a new safe house and Taylor can search for Turtle's biological relatives to hand over legal custody to her. In Oklahoma Taylor has little luck finding Turtle's relatives, but she devises a plan with Estevan and Esperanza to trick the adoption agency. The plan works, and Turtle is at last legally Taylor's daughter. They say a tearful goodbye to Estevan and Esperanza and return to Tucson a real, legal family.

Characters

Taylor

Originally named Marietta, Taylor changes her name when she leaves Pitman County, Kentucky and drives to Tucson, Arizona. The protagonist and narrator of the story, Taylor is

Turtle

An Indian three-year-old given to Taylor at a small restaurant off the highway in Oklahoma. Turtle was abused before she wound up with Taylor; as a result, she is about a year behind developmentally. She loves to learn about plant and flower names.

Sandi

A woman Taylor meets in Tucson who works at the Burger Derby. Sandi has an obsession with horses. She helps Taylor get a job at the restaurant as well, but Taylor quits after just six days.

Lou Ann

Another Kentuckian in Arizona, Lou Ann meets Taylor after putting out a roommate ad in the paper. She invites Taylor into her home, and they become fast friends. Lou Ann is a divorced young mother who worries about everything.

Mattie

The owner of Jesus Is Lord Used Tires. Mattie is the first person Taylor meets in Tucson. She is also an outspoken supporter of illegal immigrants.

Estevan

A Guatemalan refugee, Estevan entered the US illegally and lives above Mattie's tire store for protection. He is kind and handsome, and Taylor begins to like him as more than just friends.

Esperanza

Estevan's wife, Esperanza also lives above the tire store. She is quiet and withdrawn and attempts suicide because of the trauma she experienced in Guatemala. She has a strange fascination with Turtle.

Angel

Lou Ann's ex-husband, Angel is a Mexican rodeo man. After he loses his leg in a terrible car accident, his personality changes so much that he no longer seems recognizable to Lou Ann as the man with whom she fell in love.

Newt Hardbine

A boy Taylor's age from Pittman County. Newt is shot and killed while Taylor is employed at the local hospital. The experience has a profound impact on Taylor.

Alice Greer

Taylor's mother. Alice always supports Taylor to break the mold and go for her dreams. The only time they have some tension is when Alice decides to remarry with a man from Pittman County.

Themes

Family

Taylor leaves Pittman County with her mother's support, but she soon learns that family is not only biological. By the end of the novel, Taylor learns that family is what you make of it. It is the people who care most about you and are there for you no matter what. Taylor has made a new family in Tucson with Lou Ann, Dwayne Ray, and Turtle. Although they sometimes have hardships, they've seen each other at their worst and best and know that they will always love each other.

Adventure

Taylor's spirit of adventure is what leads her to begin her road trip from Kentucky in the first place. Taylor yearns to see new things and experience life outside of her small hometown. She goes out into the world with a fresh perspective and almost no preparation. Although she is faced with her fair share of surprises and setbacks, Taylor ultimately succeeds in building a home for herself in the unknown.

Immigration

Illegal immigration and the moral arguments surrounding it are an undertone of the entire novel. Mattie hides illegal immigrants from Latin America above her tire shop because they face potential torture and death if they are discovered and deported back to their home countries. Through Mattie and the people she protects, Taylor learns more about the flaws in the American immigration system and the hardships that illegal immigrants face when they make the decision to cross into the United States. The novel brings to light issues of human rights that often get overlooked in the immigration debate.

Facing Fears

Over the course of her journey, Taylor ultimately has to learn to overcome her fears and be brave even when she doesn't feel strong enough to do so. Taylor's fears range from the absurd (a phobia of exploding tires) to the profound (a fear of losing custody of Turtle or of Estevan being sent back to danger in Guatemala). Valid or not, all of Taylor's fears threaten her chances of happiness and success in Tucson. But with the support of her friends, Taylor meets her fears head on and learns that sometimes the only thing to do is carry on.

Growing Up

In many ways, *The Bean Trees* may be read as a coming of age novel. Taylor leaves Kentucky as one person and settles into Tucson life as somebody entirely different. Her transformation is marked by an evolution in maturity. Taylor has many eyeopening moments in which she discovers that the world is both more sensational and more terrible than she could have ever imagined in Kentucky. This knowledge has a massive effect on Taylor. She begins to grow into adulthood's challenges and responsibilities with a surprising strength of will.

Motherhood

When a chance encounter with a woman at a roadside restaurant leaves Taylor with a three-year-old Indian girl to take care of, she is overwhelmed and confused. However, Taylor quickly comes to love the Indian girl, who Taylor calls Turtle, as her own. Although she rarely knows the right thing to do and has plenty of mishaps along the way, Taylor develops a strong bond with Turtle as strong as that between any mother and daughter. Through her experiences, she learns that motherhood has less to do with a biological bond as it does with a bond of love and protection. A mother cannot promise to shield her child from the hardships of the world forever; what she can do, however, is promise to love that child as much as possible and give her as many opportunities as she can.

The Importance of Environment

Turtle has a strange fascination with plant and vegetable names, so much so that Taylor calls her a horticulture genius toward the end of the novel. The natural theme is present throughout the novel in other ways as well: Mattie shows Taylor purple bean vines that have been growing for over half a century, Edna and Virgie Mae point out a flower that blooms only one night a year, and Taylor goes out with Mattie and several others to witness the astounding sight of the first rainstorm of the season. The frequent references to nature in the novel compare human and natural environments and stress the importance of surroundings in development of identity.

Gender Roles

As a young woman, Taylor is distinctly aware of the difficulties of being a woman in a man's world. Most of the girls her age had teen pregnancies and got married at a young age. Not wanting to be trapped in that sort of patriarchal cycle, Taylor sets out on her own for better things outside of Kentucky. When she meets Turtle and sees the abuses the little girl has experienced, Taylor is reminded yet again of the perils of being female. And when she first moves in with Lou Ann and begins working at the tire shop, Taylor is unsettled by the ways in which her domestic patterns with Lou Ann resemble a husband-wife relationship. Although she does not ultimately break down all the gender problems she discovers, Taylor's recognition of such issues and discomfort with the status quo brings to light the gender problems in her society.

Unrequited Love

Both Lou Ann and Taylor fall in love with men they cannot have. Lou Ann is still not over Angel, the ex-husband who left her when she was seven months pregnant with their first child. And Taylor cannot seem to get over her crush on Estevan, the handsome and kind Guatemalan man living above Mattie's tire shop. But Estevan is already married, and Angel is not going to change his mind about Lou Ann. Together the two women learn that sometimes no matter how bad you want something to happen, it's not always meant to be.

Hard Work

Taylor knows from an early age that nothing in life comes easily. In high school, she takes initiative to get a job as a lab assistant at a local health clinic. When she leaves Kentucky and gets stuck with Turtle, she learns that motherhood takes a lot of hard work, as well. And Taylor's determination is tested even more when a child services agency threatens to take Turtle away from her. Throughout everything, Taylor learns that taking enormous risks can sometimes result in even greater rewards. Just because something is challenging, does not mean it is impossible or unachievable.

Chapter Summaries

Chapter 1- The One To Get Away

Chapter 1 begins with the narrator, Missy, explaining her fear of exploding tires. Missy once saw an overfilled tractor tire blow up in her small town. The force of the air was so much that it threw Newt Hardbine's father over the top of the Standard Oil sign. He lost his hearing and was never quite the same again after.

Missy's real name is Marietta, but everyone in her town in Kentucky calls her Missy. Most girls in Missy's town get pregnant at a young age and drop out of school, but Missy is determined not to end up like that. Not only does she stay in school, but thanks to a tip from her high school English teacher she also manages to get a part-time job as a lab assistant at the local hospital.

One day when Missy is working at the hospital, Newt Hardbine gets rolled in with a fatal gunshot wound. Newt, the same guy whose father was the unfortunate victim of the exploding tire incident, was in Missy's class at school. He got a girl named Jolene pregnant and then married her. He was shot as a result of domestic violence.

Missy works at the job at the hospital for over five years but eventually decides to leave the world she knows in Kentucky. She buys a '55 Volkswagen bug and leaves town by herself. When Missy crosses the Pitman County border she makes two promises to herself: the first is that she will give herself a new name, and the second is that she will drive until her car breaks down and stay wherever that may be. Missy keeps the former promise but not the latter. She passes by a place called Taylorville and decides to go by the name Taylor Greer.

The second promise, Taylor doesn't keep. This has to do with the fact that her car gives out in central Oklahoma, on the border of Cherokee reservation land. Taylor is actually an eighth Cherokee, but Oklahoma is so flat and featureless that she can't stand the thought of staying. Instead, Taylor finds a man named Bob Two-Two to fix her car. She goes into a roadside restaurant, where she writes a postcard to her ma and makes conversation with the Indian owner, Earl. There are some mean-looking men in the bar who make Taylor uneasy, so she grabs a quick meal and leaves soon after.

As Taylor is getting into the car, a woman comes up to her. She is carrying a baby that she says belongs to her dead sister. The Indian woman asks Taylor to take the baby, but Taylor says that if she wanted a baby, she would have stayed in Kentucky. Besides, to adopt a baby you need official papers. But the woman is insistent. She claims that this baby has no papers and that she is in danger if Taylor doesn't take her. Before Taylor can further object, she places the child in the front seat of the car and shuts the door.

Taylor is overwhelmed and has no idea what to do, but she drives on. She finds a motel. A kind old woman agrees to let Taylor and the baby stay for free. Taylor brings the baby inside and unwraps her from a lot of blankets. The baby is a girl, and she has bruises and worse on her. She looks like she has been severely abused. Taylor cleans the child and gives her a shirt to wear.

Chapter 2- New Year's Pig

Chapter two switches out of Taylor's perspective and describes the life of Lou Ann Ruiz, a Kentucky transplant who lives in Tucson. Her last name Ruiz she got from her husband Angel. Angel leaves Lou Ann on Halloween. Lou Ann is seven months pregnant.

Three years before, Angel was in a terrible car accident on Christmas day that left him with an amputated leg. The accident also changed his relationship with Lou Ann. He became meaner and more detached, and he would regularly accuse Lou Ann of cheating on him. On the Friday of Halloween, Angel packs up his belongings and moves out while Lou Ann is at the OB-GYN. At her appointment, Lou Ann's doctor warns her that she's been gaining too much weight, and the nurse gives her a pamphlet about maintaining a healthy prenatal diet. Lou Ann observes that the models on the pamphlet cover are racially diverse. She thinks about sending a copy to her mother. Even after four years, Lou Ann's mother still can't understand why she married a Mexican. Lou Ann has not yet broken the news to her mother that the baby will receive a Catholic baptism.

Lou Ann takes the bus home. She gets off at Roosevelt Park and walks by a place called Jesus Is Lord Used Tires. Next to the tire store is a porn shop called Fanny Heaven. She turns the corner and stops to do some shopping at the Lee Sing Market. The Chinese woman at the counter tells Lou Ann that the baby will be a girl. She says this every time Lou Ann comes in. Lou Ann says either way is okay by her, but she wonders if Lee Sing is right.

When Lou Ann arrives at her house, she notices that Angel has come home from work and gone out again. It takes her a few moments to realize that Angel has also taken all of his belongings with him. She is strangely fascinated by what Angel decided to claim as his belongings and what he left behind. In some ways, it says more about his personality than anything else he has done over the course of his marriage with Lou Ann.

Shocked by Angel's departure, Lou Ann has utterly forgotten that it is Halloween. When the children start arriving on her doorstep, she has no candy to offer so she hands out money instead. Late that night, exhausted and with hurting feet, Lou Ann cries her eyes out.

Chapter 3- Jesus Is Lord Used Tires

Taylor and the baby leave Oklahoma and cross the state line into Arizona. Taylor is amazed by the desert scenery, which seems to her to be too goofy to be real. She stayed in the Oklahoma motel through the Christmas holidays, helping out with the housekeeping in return for free rent. But after the New Year Taylor decided it was time to move on.

Taylor has taken to calling the Indian child Turtle on account of the way she grabs onto everything. The baby doesn't speak at all and hardly seems to react to anything. The innkeeper Mrs. Hoge thought she was retarded, but Taylor thinks the child just has her own way of doing things.

As Taylor and Turtle reach Tucson, it begins to hail and then rain. Taylor pulls over from the storm, only to discover that she has two flat tires. Fortunately, she has ended up right by a tire store: Jesus Is Lord Used Tires. Taylor brings Turtle inside the store and talks to the owner, a woman named Mattie. Mattie says the flats are too bad to patch and that Taylor will need entirely new tires. Taylor says that's fine, even though she doesn't have the money to pay for it. Mattie offers Taylor coffee and Turtle apple juice. She warns Taylor that kids can dehydrate in the desert heat, even in the winter. Mattie also shows Taylor and Turtle some bean vines she has outside. The vines were planted from seeds that the Chinese lady next door brought over in 1907. The same plant has been going all these years.

Taylor decides she will stay in Tucson and begins renting by the week at the Hotel Republic. Tucson is a lively city that feels different from anything else Taylor's seen on her trip or in her life, in Pittman County. There are all different types of people, including secretary and lawyer types along with prostitutes and artsy individuals who lived on the streets.

Taylor meets a woman named Sandi who works at a restaurant called the Burger Derby. Taylor eats there regularly so she can hang out with Sandi and have some company. Sandi is crazy about horses, so when she finds out Taylor is from Kentucky, she gets terribly excited and goes on and on about the Kentucky Derby. Taylor tries to explain to Sandi that not everyone in Kentucky owns a thoroughbred, but it's a lost cause.

The Burger Derby is hiring, so Taylor asks Sandi what it's like to work there. Sandi says it's fantastic. She has a child just like Taylor, and she leaves him at a daycare center at the mall. The daycare is free and designed for women shopping, but Sandi just checks in every two hours and no one seems to notice or care that she's not actually at the mall. Sandi then asks about Turtle, saying that no offense, but Turtle and Taylor look nothing alike. Taylor explains that Turtle isn't actually her daughter, just somebody she kind of got stuck with. Sandi looks thoughtful and says that she knows exactly what Taylor means.

Chapter 4- Tug Fork Water

Chapter four switches back to Lou Ann, whose mother and grandmother have come to visit. They came all the way from Kentucky to Tucson, traveling three days on a Greyhound bus. They have come to see Dwayne Ray, the little boy that Lou Ann gave birth to. Even though Angel left Lou Ann, he agreed to move back in for her family's visit. Lou Ann realizes that Angel must recognize the power of mothers and grandmothers. She has not told Granny Logan or her mother Ivy that she and Angel might get a divorce. This would only justify all their prejudices against Angel, and they would ask Lou Ann to move back home.

Granny Logan is cranky, complaining about everything from the heat to the bed she slept in. She is also not speaking with Ivy because they are fighting about something or other as usual. Lou Ann asks her mother if she and Lou Ann's daddy always lived with Granny Logan. Ivy says that they did. She would have been scared to death to go off and live somewhere on her own like Lou Ann has done in Tucson.

Granny Logan tells Lou Ann that she talks different now, and that Tucson is making her put on airs and forget her Kentucky roots. She also badmouths Angel, saying it's a sin that he works on Sundays. Granny Logan then gives Lou Ann a bottle of muddy water. The water came from Tug Fork Creek, the small river where Lou Ann's entire family was baptized. She instructs Lou Ann to use the water for Dwayne Ray's baptism.

Lou Ann sees her mother and grandmother to the bus stop, where they offer some last words of guidance and Granny Logan complains some more. After her family leaves, Lou Ann decides to buy some tomatoes from a man named Bobby Bingo who sells vegetables out of his truck. Bingo talks about his son, who apparently is famous and does Cadillac commercials on TV. He used to wish that his son would be somebody significant, but now he barely acknowledges Bingo's existence. Bingo warns Lou Ann that the precise thing you want can end up being the worst thing for you.

Back at the house Lou Ann keeps repeating "the worst thing for you" under her breath. She nurses Dwayne Ray in the front room until Angel returns home from work. Angel goes into the kitchen, and Lou Ann notices that his presence feels different than when her mother and grandmother were in the house. Unlike the women, his presence seems neutral. It hardly makes a difference to her whether he is there or not. Angel asks Lou Ann if she has seen a few of his belongings that he wants to pack and take with him. He then notices the bottle of water from Tug Fork Creek. When Lou Ann says her grandmother brought it for Dwayne Ray's baptism, Angel pours the water down the drain.

Chapter 5 - Harmonious Space

The Republic Hotel is located right next to Tucson's railroad track. The trains whistle around 6:15 every morning, and Taylor comes to use their noise as her alarm clock. She and Turtle are in trouble financially because Taylor has been unable to keep a job. Taylor was hired at the Burger Derby, where she lasted a total of six days before she quit and stormed out. The cause of her outrage was a manager named Jerry Speller who thought his position made him better than everyone else. Taylor was annoyed that the uniforms were dry-clean only and that the restaurant wouldn't pay for the cleaning. Jerry told Taylor she didn't have the right attitude for the job. Taylor agreed with him, and that was that.

Although Taylor is glad not to be working at the Burger Derby under such a jerk, the downside is that she doesn't see Sandi as much since she can't exactly show her face in the restaurant anymore. The other downside, of course, is that Taylor has no steady income. To offset the expense of living at the Republic Hotel, Taylor begins to search the local paper for roommate ads. She finds two options that sound promising. The first asks for a roommate open to new ideas, and the second is from a single mom looking for company. The former sounds adventurous and the second comfortable.

At the first house, Taylor meets three roommates who wear toe rings and say that caffeine disrupts your homeostasis. They interrogate Taylor about her lifestyle and say that they have a soymilk collective. Each housemate is responsible for at least seven hours a week straining curd. The second house visit goes much better. The house belongs to a woman named Lou Ann. Not only is Lou Ann also from Kentucky, but she and Taylor also discover that their hometowns are separated by only two counties. Lou Ann and Taylor connect right away, and are soon laughing away about their lives and swapping story about their respective babies. Lou Ann says it's been a long time since she met someone who talked just like her.

Chapter 6 - Valentine's Day

On Valentine's Day, the first killing frost of the winter comes to Tucson. Mattie listened to the weather forecast the night before the frost and took in her tomatoes to make green tomato pie. Taylor is sad to see that the frost has destroyed some of the other vegetables in the garden, but Mattie tells Taylor that's just the cycle of life.

Taylor has taken a job at Jesus Is Lord Used Tires. Even though she was broke, Taylor didn't want the job at first on account of her fear of exploding tires. Mattie wore her down though, and even after Taylor told her about her fear, she didn't laugh. Mattie explained to Taylor that a tire's air pressure only had the power to knock the wind out of you. When Taylor told the story of watching Newt Hardbine's father thrown over the gas sign in Pittman County, Mattie says that he was using a tractor tire, and not a normal one. This put Taylor a little more at ease and she agreed to the job.

Mattie's place is always bustling with different people passing through. Many of these people are not customers either. A lot of Spanish-speaking people come and stay in the rooms above the tire store for varying amounts of time. They are often accompanied by a blue jeans wearing priest named Father William. Father Williams and Mattie talk privately for long periods of time whenever he shows up.

Meanwhile, Taylor and Turtle are settling into life with Lou Ann and Dwayne Ray. Taylor decides to buy Turtle a book about Old MacDonald growing vegetables in an apartment building. Lou Ann buys a book of baby names and begins to read it aloud to Turtle in hopes that she'll respond. She thinks Turtle isn't an appropriate name and is on a quest to find her a new one. Lou Ann is worried that Turtle lacks personality. Taylor claims that Turtle has plenty of personality. Her personality just happens to be grabbing onto things.

Taylor is in a bad mood, but she doesn't realize why until after the kids are in bed. The reason she is unhappy is that she feels like she and Lou Ann have a married-couple relationship. Taylor goes out to work every day, while Lou Ann stays home and watches the kids and cooks dinner. Taylor brings this up to Lou Ann. They have a long talk about it. Lou Ann is drunk and upset. She says she is always afraid that if she screws up even a little bit she will lose her friends. She says that after Angel left, she kept remembering a time they had gone out with friends to see a meteor shower. Lou Ann had gotten drunk, and the next day she couldn't remember a thing. Angel kept saying that the meteor shower was unbelievable, and he couldn't believe that Lou Ann missed it. Lou Ann always wonders if that night had something to do with why Angel left her. Taylor tells her not to worry about Angel, and they settle their disagreement about their living expectations.

Chapter 7- How They Eat in Heaven

Taylor and Lou Ann go out on a picnic with Mattie, and the couple currently living above Jesus Is Lord Used Tires, Estevan and Esperanza. Estevan had been an English teacher in Guatemala City. He and his wife entered America illegally to escape prosecution. They live up in Mattie's sanctuary for the time being.

Taylor is intensely attracted to Estevan, whom she finds dark and handsome. His wife, on the other hand, is much more reserved. She is quiet and small and in some ways reminds Taylor of Turtle. There was an incident between Turtle and Esperanza earlier in the day. Esperanza kept staring at Turtle so much until eventually Taylor asked her husband Estevan if she was okay. Estevan replied that she was fine—Turtle just reminded Esperanza of a child they had known back in Guatemala, and that was all.

At the picnic, Estevan decides to go for a swim in the stream and Taylor joins him. Lou Ann, in her typical worrying fashion, swears they will get pneumonia. But Taylor doesn't care. Estevan whoops when he runs into the cold water and then starts singing in Spanish to Esperanza. Taylor is amazed by his smooth and sweet voice.

In the evening, everyone drives back in Mattie's and Taylor's cars. Estevan drives Mattie's car, and Mattie warns him not to get pulled over since he has no license and is an illegal immigrant. Estevan is a careful driver, but he slams on the breaks of Mattie's pickup truck to avoid hitting a quail crossing the road. Taylor skids to a stop behind him and there is a squeal in the backseat. Taylor freaks out that Turtle may have been hurt, but Turtle is fine. She did a summersault in the backseat, and the noise she made was a laugh. It's the first laugh Taylor has ever heard from her.

Several weeks later, Turtle says her first word: "bean." Taylor hugs her and tells her that she is the smartest little girl alive. At the end of the week, Taylor invites Estevan and Esperanza over for dinner. Lou Ann invites some neighbors named Edna Poppy and Virgie Mae Valentine Parsons. Edna and Virgie are also supposed to bring their portable TV over so Lou Ann and Taylor can see an interview with Mattie. By the time the neighbors come, they catch just the tail end of the interview. Mattie is talking with a reporter about immigration and naturalization laws. She says that two illegal aliens from El Salvador had been taken into custody in the US and the deported. According to Mattie, the two were found dead in a ditch just a week after they were forced back to El Salvador.

The neighbors Edna and Virgie Mae turn out to be rather eccentric. Edna wears only red clothing and looks at you funny when she speaks, as if there is something fascinating going on just over your head. Virgie Mae is a sour old lady. She makes a lot of rude comments about illegal immigrants right in front of Estevan and Esperanza. Taylor cringes from embarrassment. Esperanza is still fascinated by Turtle, who seems to be the only one able to make her smile. Taylor serves Chinese food for the whole crew, and they sit down to eat.

Chapter 8 - The Miracle of Dog Doo Park

Taylor's mother calls Tucson to announce that she is getting married to a man named Harland Elleston, who co-owns El-Jay's Paint and Body in Pittman County. Taylor is taken aback by the news. She complains to Lou Ann about it, but Lou Ann points out that everyone is entitled to have someone. Taylor says that her mother has her, but Lou Ann claims that doesn't count and accuses Taylor of being jealous.

The two are sitting in Roosevelt Park with Dwayne Ray and Turtle. The neighborhood kids call the park Dog Doo Park because it is filled with dead grass, dog droppings, and little shade. Turtle plays in the dirt and repeats the word cabbage over and over. Since she began talking, she has taken to saying as many vegetable names as possible. Lou Ann points out to Taylor that she hasn't exactly expressed a lot of interest in men herself. Taylor says that she likes Estevan; Lou Ann says that he's taken so Taylor needs to get over it.

Toward the end of March, Dog Doo Park starts to transform. With the coming of spring, all the trees sprout leaves and begin to blossom. Amazed at the change, Taylor calls it the Miracle of Dog Doo Park. Taylor and Lou Ann have taken to leaving their kids with Edna and Virgie Mae on a regular basis. Turtle calls Edna Ma Poppy; she calls anyone who is a girl 'Ma' something, and she calls Taylor just Ma.

Edna and Virgie Mae come up to Taylor and Lou Ann in the park. Virgie Mae informs Lou Ann that a man was looking for her around the house and said he would come back later. Lou Ann thinks the man must have been Angel and wonders what he's doing back. Taylor asks Lou Ann what would happen if Angel wanted to get back together. Lou Ann seems surprised by the question and says that, of course, she would say yes.

Taylor eventually apologizes to Estevan for Virgie Mae's rude comments about illegal immigrants the night they all had dinner together. Estevan says not to worry about it—that's just the way Americans think. He calls Taylor mi'ija, which is Spanish for "my daughter" but translates more to something like "my friend." Taylor begins to learn more about the people who seek sanctuary with Mattie: many of them have been tortured and persecuted by the governments of their home countries.

Even though Turtle seems pretty healthy, Taylor decides she needs a doctor's appointment just to be sure. She takes Turtle to see Dr. P on Lou Ann's recommendation, even though, strictly speaking, he is an OBGYN, not a pediatrician. Taylor has trouble in the doctor's office because she doesn't know any of Turtle's medical history and doesn't have any of the proper paperwork. She tells the nurse she is a foster parent, and this seems to work as a sufficient explanation. Taylor tells Dr. Pelinowsky that she suspects Turtle was sexually abused in her original home. Dr. P says that there is no physical trauma evident, but that psychological trauma can sometimes present itself later. Either way, young children can often bounce back from that sort of thing.

The real concern over Turtle's health comes when Dr. P decides to do some x-rays just to make sure she's OK. The x-rays show a series of healed bone fractures. They also show that Turtle is probably closer to three years in age, even though she looks and acts more like a two-year-old. Sometimes when children are in difficult environments, they stop developing. This condition is called failure to thrive. Taylor points out that Turtle is thriving now, and Dr. P assures her that the condition is reversible, but Taylor is still deeply concerned.

When Taylor and Turtle are done with the doctor, they meet Lou Ann and Dwayne Ray at the zoo. Lou Ann is crying because apparently Angel finally did stop by the house. He is trying to leave town and plans on joining any rodeo that wants a one-legged clown. While he is gone he may not be able to send regular childcare checks. Taylor doesn't understand what the problem is exactly, but Lou Ann explains that she doesn't think she could get a job because she has no skills. She is also hurt that Angel didn't ask her and Dwayne Ray to go with him on the rodeo. Taylor says that Angel moved out six months ago. It's April already so it's time Lou Ann moved on. When Taylor says the word "April," Turtle looks up. Lou Ann and Taylor say the word over and over in various contexts, and every time Turtle responds. This is how they learn that her real name must be April.

Chapter 9 - Ismene

Esperanza tries to kill herself one night. Estevan comes in through the back door to tell Taylor the news. She took a whole bottle of children's aspirin. Mattie found out and rushed her to a clinic she knows of where you don't have to show papers. Taylor doesn't know how to respond to this. She tells Estevan that when she gets nervous she either makes a lot of food for people or talks too much. Estevan says he's not hungry so she might as well talk.

Taylor chops carrots for Turtle's lunch the next day. She rattles on about various unimportant things—the family reunion Lou Ann is currently attending, the different social groups that existed in her high school. She tells Estevan that the poor farm kids such as herself were called Nutters and were at the bottom of the social chain. Estevan likens this to the Untouchables in the Indian caste system.

Taylor mentions a boy from high school named Scotty who killed himself on his sixteenth boyfriend. She thinks it's because he didn't fit into any of the groups. But with Esperanza it's different—she had Estevan. Taylor realizes that she is angry with Esperanza for what happened. Out of nowhere, Estevan tells Taylor that, in Guatemala, they use electricity from old-fashioned telephones to torture people during interrogation. Taylor is shocked by this revelation and ashamed that she was blabbering about such silly things when Estevan and Esperanza have experienced real danger and trauma.

Turtle wakes up and gets out of bed. Taylor tells her to go back to sleep. Turtle hops backwards down the hall in an adorable way that makes both Taylor and Estevan laugh relieving some of the tension in the room. Estevan explains that the reason Esperanza was so drawn to Turtle that day in the park is that Turtle looks remarkably like their daughter, Ismene. Estevan was a member of a teacher's union in Guatemala that the government oppressed. In a raid on his neighborhood, the police killed several union members including Esperanza's brother. They also abducted Ismene. Soon after the raid, Estevan and Esperanza escaped to the United States.

When Taylor asks why they didn't try to go after Ismene, Estevan explains that that is exactly what the government wanted. Estevan and Esperanza knew the names of 17 other union members. To attempt to get their daughter back, they would have to forfeit the lives of all those other people. Taylor starts to cry at the realization that she lives in a world where people have to make such terrible choices. Turtle shows up in the doorway again, and Taylor cuddles with her a little bit before sending her back to bed. Taylor and Estevan talk some more and eventually fall asleep on the couch. Taylor wakes up with Estevan curled around her like spoons. She thinks of Esperanza and all she's gone through and gently slides off the sofa to sleep in her own room.

Chapter 10 - The Bean Trees

Things always look different in the morning. Mattie calls with the news that Esperanza will be just fine—they didn't even need to pump her stomach. Taylor makes breakfast for Estevan and then sends him home before she can fall in love with him even more. Lou Ann comes back from her family reunion in a good mood. She and Taylor are gradually changing the house to make it more homely and kid friendly. Lou Ann is also getting more serious about her job hunt. Turtle is speaking more and more and seems as happy as ever. In the park, she sees wisteria plants and calls them 'bean trees.'

Taylor goes out with Turtle to Lee Sing's Market to buy groceries. There they run into Edna, who is walking with a white cane. Virgie Mae is home sick, and it is the first time Taylor has seen Edna alone. Edna asks Taylor whether she is holding lemons or limes in her hand. With a shock, Taylor realizes that Edna is blind. This explains why she only wears red and why Virgie Mae holds onto her when she walks and always announces the names of people in the room. Taylor shares the news with Lou Ann when she returns home. They are both amazed they never noticed before.

On Monday afternoon, Taylor asks Mattie if she can go upstairs to visit Esperanza. She has never been upstairs before and is surprised by how cramped it is. Every surface seems to be covered, and there are many things that must have belonged to Mattie's dead husband. Esperanza sits in a chair by the window in one of the bedrooms. Taylor asks her how she is feeling. Esperanza nods and looks at her hands. Taylor tells Esperanza that she has a beautiful name—Estevan told Taylor that it means both hope and to wait in Spanish. Taylor encourages Esperanza not to give up hope and to think of reasons to stick it out. Esperanza nods again, but she doesn't make eye contact or say anything. It seems like Esperanza is not actually there, kind of like Turtle was at first.

Chapter 11 - Dream Angels

Toward the end of May, Lou Ann gets a job at Red Hot Mama's salsa factory. The factory has long hours, low pay, and employees often have to be careful about touching their eyes or privates because the juice from the hot peppers makes their hands sting. Despite all this, Lou Ann loves the job. She brings home salsa samples and incorporates them into all her dinner recipes. She also lectures Taylor endlessly on the merits of salsa including its sinus-clearing effects. Taylor is so sick of salsa that when it is her turn to cook, she takes to making the blandest foods she can think of to offset the spice.

Since Lou Ann and Taylor are both working now, they leave the kids with Edna and Virgie Mae more and more often. For a while, Lou Ann is afraid to say anything to Edna because she is so embarrassed for not knowing she was blind. Finally, Taylor tells Edna why Lou Ann is acting so weird, and Edna says she is flattered they didn't even realize.

There hasn't been any rain since the frost in February, and the heat is getting to everyone. The whole world seems to be drying up. Lou Ann tells Taylor that when Dwayne Ray was born she had a dream that an angel came to her and told her that he would die before the year 2000. She also read a horoscope and some other signs that indicated the same thing. Lou Ann is so terrified of Dwayne Ray dying that she sees potential disasters in everything. Taylor points out that the flip side of worrying too much is not caring enough. If anything, Lou Ann's paranoia makes her a better mother.

In June Angel sends a package with gifts for Lou Ann and Dwayne Ray. He writes that he has changed his mind about the divorce and wants Lou Ann to come live with him in Montana. Lou Ann is amazed that Angel actually misses her. But she has responsibilities now: she has been promoted to manager at Red Hot Mama's. Still, Taylor feels in her bones that Lou Ann will eventually give in and follow Angel to Montana. The last time Taylor talked to Mattie, she said that tensions were rising by the border about immigration. Mattie wants to move Esperanza and Estevan to another state before they are discovered. Mattie is extremely bitter about the US response to illegal immigrants. Taylor feels like everything is changing extremely fast.

Chapter 12 - Into the Terrible Night

At three o'clock one afternoon, the cicadas that live behind Mattie's tire shop stop buzzing. By four o'clock, there is thunder: rain is finally coming to Tucson. Mattie closes down the shop for the afternoon and takes Taylor, Esperanza, and Estevan out in her truck to see the rain. Taylor calls Edna and Virgie Mae to ask if they can watch Turtle a little later than usual. Mattie explains that the indigenous peoples who lived in the desert long ago used to celebrate the New Year on the day of the summer's first rain. She tells Taylor that she'll see why soon enough.

Mattie drives everyone on a gravel road to an overlook where you can see all of Tucson Valley. From their vantage point, they can physically see the storm coming. A huge mass of clouds moves in from the south, and Taylor can make out lightning in the distance. The storm picks up speed, and in what feels like an instant, the rain is upon the truck. The downpour is incredible. The thunder sounds like music, and everyone laughs and dances in the rain. The rain has a strong smell that is hard to describe but seems musty somehow. It's dark by the time the foursome head back to Mattie's truck.

When Taylor gets back home she can tell right away that something's wrong. Lou Ann looks like she's been crying and she isn't even supposed to be home yet. Taylor asks what's wrong, and Lou Ann says she's so sorry, but it's Turtle. Taylor runs inside. Edna is sitting on the couch with Turtle on her lap. Turtle looks OK physically, but her eyes are darker and she looks detached, like she used to be when Taylor first found her. Taylor demands to know what happened, but nobody is entirely sure. Edna and Turtle were out on a walk in the park. Being blind, Edna didn't notice it was getting dark. Turtle stopped singing and then Edna heard a strange noise and the sounds of a struggle. She swung with her cane and hit something, or more like someone. The next thing she knew Turtle was grabbing her leg as tight as she could.

There is a knock on the door—Virgie Mae has called the police, and they come with a social worker to talk to Turtle. The social worker gives Turtle some anatomically correct dolls. She explains to Taylor that children don't always have the vocabulary to talk about what happened to them so they use the dolls. If Turtle's been molested, she will talk about it eventually. Taylor disagrees. She thinks Turtle will never talk again. All the progress she's made seems to be gone in an instant. Taylor can't bear to go to Turtle while she's in that state, so she goes around the house chasing a bird that's gotten in instead.

The medical examiner says there is no evidence that Taylor was molested. She was probably just shaken up by the incident. But it's been days, and Turtle still hasn't said a word. Taylor feels like she just spent eight months trying to convince Turtle that no one would hurt her again only to break her promise. Lou Ann says you can't promise a thing like that to a kid. You can only promise to take care of her as much as you are able. She is angry with Taylor for not going to comfort Turtle that first night, but Taylor doesn't want to talk about it. Taylor stops sleeping at night, and Mattie spends a vast deal of time trying to convince Edna, Virgie, and Taylor respectively that it wasn't their fault. Taylor starts noticing homeless people on the street and thinks that things are so wrong for so many people. Lou Ann tries to remind her that you have to fight back; nothing gets better on its own.

Chapter 13- Night Blooming Cereus

Turtle turns out to be resilient after all. Within a few weeks, she is talking again. She never does anything with the anatomically correct dolls, but she does occasionally mention the 'bad man' that Ma Poppy hit with her cane. Taylor and Turtle start seeing the social worker, Cynthia, twice a week. Cynthia spends a lot of time talking with the two of them about the traumas Turtle experienced before she came to Taylor. Cynthia is not shocked by what happened to Turtle and says that up to 1 little girl in 4 is abused by a family member. This saddens Taylor, but she reasons that at least Turtle is not alone should she ever want to talk about it some day.

Cynthia also brings Taylor the unwelcome news that she has no legal right to take care of Turtle. Unless Taylor can prove that she didn't kidnap Turtle or force the parents to give her up, Turtle could become a ward of the state. Taylor has only two or three weeks before someone from Child Protection Services contacts her about Turtle's custody.

Lou Ann has a fit when she hears the news. She is furious that anyone would try to take Turtle away from Taylor. But Taylor isn't sure what to think. She doesn't want to lose Turtle, but then again, she's not sure she's prepared to be the mother Turtle deserves, especially after everything that's happened in the past few weeks. Lou Ann thinks Taylor is giving up too easily and is now angry with Taylor, as well.

Mattie offers some perspective by reminding Taylor that most laws have loopholes so she shouldn't think the situation is doomed just yet. Taylor asks Mattie to think back to when Taylor first arrived in Tucson. Did Taylor look like a decent parent? Mattie says Taylor looked like a bewildered parent, which is how any new mother looks. Taylor wants to know how a person is supposed to make such a momentous decision as whether or not to be a parent. Mattie says that most people don't get to decide; parenthood just happens to them.

The next time Taylor meets with Cynthia she goes without Turtle. She doesn't like talking about Turtle's custody in her presence because she knows Turtle understands more than she lets on. She asks Cynthia all about adoption laws and documentation. She discovers there may be some exceptions to having a birth certificate if a child is born on an Indian reservation. Cynthia also gives her the information of a lawyer in Oklahoma who may be able to help her case. Taylor is surprised to discover that Cynthia has been on her side the whole time—she never had any doubt that Turtle belonged with Taylor rather than the state.

That night Taylor can't sleep at all, but, by morning, she's made up her mind. She will drive to Oklahoma to try to find a relative of Turtle's to legally hand over custody. During the trip, she will also transport Estevan and Esperanza across state lines so that they can go to a new safe house in Oklahoma. The night before Taylor is supposed to leave, Virgie Mae knocks on the door. She says there is something she wants to show Taylor, Lou Ann, and the kids. Edna is sitting on the porch next to a plant with the most magnificent blossoms Taylor has ever seen. Virgie explains that the plant is a night-blooming cereus, and its flowers only come out one night in the entire year. Lou Ann thinks the plant is a sign of good luck.

If the plant is a sign of anything, it is of exceptional weather. The sky is beautiful the next day when Taylor, Turtle, Estevan, and Esperanza set out to leave. They are taking Mattie's truck, and several people have come to see them off. Mattie hands Taylor some money and reminds her to be careful—the consequences of transporting illegal immigrants are up to 5 years in prison. Taylor starts the engine and their trip begins.

Chapter 14- Guardian Saints

Immigration officers stop the car about 100 miles before the New Mexico border. It is just a routine check, but Taylor is still so nervous she could burst. The immigration officer asks if everyone in the car is a U.S. citizen, and Taylor responds yes. But then the man asks whose kid it is. Taylor hesitates for a second and turns to Estevan, who responds that the child is theirs. The officer nods and waves everyone through. After, Estevan apologizes for claiming Turtle was his child. But he didn't know what else to do because Taylor hesitated. Taylor knows Estevan did the right thing, but it still bothers her a bit. She is also bothered by the fact that Turtle has taken to calling Esperanza just 'Ma.' Taylor knows she is being ridiculous since there's no way Turtle could pronounce Esperanza, but she still feels jealous.

For most of the trip, Taylor makes conversation with Estevan in the front seat while Esperanza plays with Turtle in the back. Estevan talks about Guatemala and they all play word games to keep themselves from going crazy from boredom. In Oklahoma Taylor stops at the Broken Arrow Motor Lodge where she had spent the holidays the previous year. There she discovers that Mrs. Hoge passed away not long after she left in January. The next morning she has to decide whether she will take Esperanza and Estevan to their new sanctuary first or whether she will bring them to look for Turtle's family. The former choice is safer for the couple, but the latter means they can spend more time with Taylor and Turtle. The couple chooses to stay with Taylor.

Taylor wasn't sure she would remember the exact restaurant where she was given Turtle, but she recognizes it right away. Estevan gives Taylor a hug for courage. Then Esperanza does, then Turtle. Taylor goes inside the restaurant. It looks different, and a teenage girl greets her. The restaurant has switched ownership, and the girl knows nothing about the people who had it before or who may have come by often. Taylor is no closer to finding Turtle's relatives. The girl does show Taylor some postcards of beautiful lakes and mountains on the nearby Cherokee reservation.

Taylor thought that maybe once she started driving again she would have a solution, but when she pulls away from the restaurant she has no idea what to do. Still, she knows she has come too far to give up just yet. Taylor tells Estevan and Esperanza that she wants to go to Lake o' the Cherokees, although she isn't sure why. She asks them again if they would rather be dropped off at the safe house first, but they want to go to the lake too. Taylor says they will have a picnic there. It will be like a little vacation—no one in the car has ever had a vacation before.

Chapter 15 - Lake o' the Cherokees

As Taylor drives through the Cherokee Nation, she notices that there are fewer and fewer white people in sight. She realizes that this must be the first time in a very long time that Estevan and Esperanza have looked like they belong. The transformation is evident—they both look more relaxed than Taylor has ever seen them. The scenery grows more appealing also, with more trees and hills. At one point, Turtle shouts "mama" and points out the window. It is the first time Taylor has ever heard her refer to anyone as mama. All she can see out the window are a gas station and a cemetery.

Lake o' the Cherokees is more beautiful than Taylor could have imagined. They find a beautiful cottage right away, and Taylor uses the money Mattie gave her to pay for a night. She convinces Estevan and Esperanza that they are entitled to have a delightful time for just one night. They all sit out by the lake and Turtle names the flowers for them. Something in Esperanza is changing here. She seems livelier than Taylor has ever seen her, and when she holds Turtle she seems genuinely happy. Turtle is supposed to be calling Estevan and Esperanza by their English names Steven and Hope so that they can get used to hearing it. But she tells them that she likes their original names too much. Besides, with everything else in their life changed, they deserve to keep something constant.

Later they find a place that rents boats. Esperanza doesn't want to go so she stays behind with Turtle while Taylor and Estevan go out on the lake. Estevan takes off his shirt and looks perfect in the sun. Taylor can't help but think that she has never wanted anyone as much as she wants Estevan in this moment. She tells him that she will miss him an incredible amount when he leaves. Estevan doesn't say he will miss Taylor. They both know this is a conversation they can't afford to get into at the moment.

At sunset, they find picnic tables for a picnic. Turtle buries her dolls in the dirt, which is a habit of hers. Taylor explains to Turtle that the dolls won't grow anything when they're buried. Beans and seeds grow plants; babies don't. Turtle says yes, but then she pats the mound and says "mama" for the second time that day. With a start, Taylor realizes that Turtle must be remembering her real mother who died. That's why she said, "mama," when she saw the cemetery. It is one of many times with Turtle that Taylor has no idea what to do. She tells Turtle she is sorry and begins to cry. Later that night Taylor has an idea. She tells Estevan and Esperanza that she has a favor to ask them, but it will be dangerous for them so she wants them to think quite hard on it before they agree. She says they don't have to say yes, but when Estevan and Esperanza hear what Taylor has planned they agree right away.

Chapter 16 - Soundness of Mind and Freedom of Will

Taylor goes to see Mr. Armistead, the Oklahoma lawyer that Cynthia the social worker recommended. Estevan and Esperanza come with her. They are pretending to be Turtle's biological parents so that Taylor can have a legal adoption. Estevan is an incredibly talented liar. He makes up all sorts of convincing details about his life as an Oklahoma Cherokee. But the most convincing of everyone is Esperanza. She holds Turtle tightly with tears in her eyes and tells Mr. Armistead that they love Turtle very much, but they move around too much to care for her. Esperanza starts crying for real, and Taylor realizes that this is not just an act for her. Estevan adds that it is hard, but they know Turtle will be happy with Taylor and grow to have a warm heart.

It takes what seems like forever, but finally Mr. Armistead's secretary Mrs. Cleary types up a legal statement for the adoption. The statement says that Taylor will be the sole parent and guardian for April Turtle. Everyone signs the document in the presence of witnesses. As everyone files out, Taylor can see the relief on Estevan's face that everything worked out. He and Esperanza both wore clothing that was kind of shabby since Taylor told them that if they wore their best clothing the lawyer might not believe that Turtle was better off without them. She hates that Estevan and Esperanza had to sacrifice their pride for her, but that's how awful she wants Turtle.

Chapter 17- Rhizobia

Taylor originally thought maybe the cemetery they passed was the actual cemetery that Turtle's mother was buried in. But they have passed several cemeteries now, and Turtle shouts "mama" at every one. Taylor finds the church where Estevan and Esperanza will be living. Taylor says goodbye to Esperanza in a daze and is left outside the church with just Estevan. She tells Estevan she is worried about him being stuck there and what will happen to him. Estevan says he will survive, and Taylor starts to cry. She says that when Esperanza said goodbye to Turtle back in the adoption office it was like she was saying goodbye to Ismene, her real daughter, instead. Estevan agrees that Esperanza had some sort of cathartic moment and now seems able to let her daughter go. Estevan kisses Taylor sweetly and goes into the house.

Taylor calls her mother from a payphone at a gas station. She feels sorry that she hasn't called her mother in two months since hearing the news about her getting remarried. But now she can't stop crying. Taylor tells her mother how she just said goodbye to a man she loved. She also tells her mother that Turtle is now going to be hers legally. Her mom is thrilled, and Taylor thanks her for being so good and supportive when Taylor was growing up. Her mother says one of these days she and Harland will come out to Arizona to visit. Neither woman wants to hang up, and they say goodbye about three times before they actually do.

On an impulse, Taylor calls 1-800-THE LORD. Taylor's not sure exactly why she does it after seeing that number so many times before. The woman who answers the phone asks if what amount Taylor would like to pledge to the Fountain of Faith missionary fund. Taylor says she doesn't have a pledge; she just wants to thank the woman for getting her through some difficult times. No matter what, she always knew she could call 1-800-THE LORD if she truly needed. This bewilders the woman on the other end of the line.

Taylor takes Turtle to a public library in Oklahoma where they look at books together. Turtle's favorite book is the Horticulture Encyclopedia. Taylor reads to her about wisteria vines. Their secret is a microscopic bug called Rhizobia that lives in the ground and fertilizes the soil for the vines. Taylor likes the idea that there is a whole invisible system helping the plant out that you don't even know is there.

At four o'clock Taylor and Turtle return to the courthouse to pick up the papers. Even though Taylor knows remarkably little can go wrong or be reversed at this point, she is still nervous. To distract herself from waiting, Taylor calls Lou Ann. Lou Ann is thrilled to hear from her and even more thrilled to discover that Taylor gets to keep Taylor. She also informs Taylor that she is over Angel for good and has started dating a charming man named Cameron who also works at Red Hot Mama's. Lou Ann also says that someone asked her about her family and she referred to Taylor, Turtle, and Dwayne Ray as her family without thinking. Taylor realizes that they have indeed become a little family.

By sundown, Taylor and Turtle are out of Oklahoma City and back on the road headed to Tucson. Taylor lets Turtle see the adoption certificate and explains that this means that Turtle is officially her kid. Turtle nods and seems to understand this. Taylor also says that from now on she is the only Ma. Lou Ann is just Lou Ann, and Edna is just Poppy. Turtle starts singing a vegetable soup song; only she puts people in the ingredients list, as well. Lou Ann, Mattie, Esperanza and all the rest are included. But Taylor is the main ingredient.

About BookCaps

We all need refreshers every now and then. Whether you are a student trying to cram for that big final, or someone just trying to understand a book more, BookCaps can help. We are a small, but growing company, and are adding titles every month.

Visit www.bookcaps.com to see more of our books, or contact us with any questions.

Made in the USA
Lexington, KY
11 July 2016